JULY 2011

Strategic Cutback Management: Law Enforcement Leadership for Lean Times

NCJ 232077

ABOUT THIS REPORT

The United States is experiencing the 10th economic decline since World War II. This document presents lessons learned from past experience and suggests approaches leaders can use to address financial crises in law enforcement agencies.

Leadership is the most critical element for success. We know from the past that an organization's leaders create a shared sense of the importance of the priorities and tasks of the group. It is this inspiration that induces workers to follow along in support of the group's mission.

Additional lessons learned from the past:

- **Avoid across-the-board cuts.** They cause disproportionate harm.

- **Use the crisis to improve management and improve productivity.** In law enforcement, examples abound of departments faced with unfortunate crises — from consent decrees to accidental shootings — where the events provided meaningful moments of reflection, learning and process improvement. Budget crises are no different.

- **Think long term.** Research has shown that organizations capable of enduring a deep fiscal crisis had developed and were able to stick to a strategic plan with a multiyear time frame.

- **Do not just cut costs, look for revenue opportunities.** Research on past recessions shows that increasing a tax or fee provides relief faster than cutting expenditures. Although police agencies do not have the power to levy taxes, they may be able to charge user fees for some services.

- **Invite innovation.** During past fiscal crises, new approaches were tried that are now standard in many cities. For example, local governments have privatized certain city services and sold public facility naming rights.

- **Look outside for help.** Law enforcement can look outside the department to other government agencies, or to suppliers, academics or other subject-matter experts for suggestions on improving operations at reduced cost.

- **Targeted layoffs are more effective than hiring freezes.**

Jane Wiseman

Strategic Cutback Management: Law Enforcement Leadership for Lean Times

Is it possible to manage well during an economic decline? Is it possible to actually improve operations instead of just trying to do more with less? The answer to both questions is "yes."

Although the current economic picture is bleak, executives still have options that allow them to manage well, and in some cases to actually improve operations.

This document presents alternatives to across-the-board, slash-and-burn budget cutting. It provides police departments with practical tools for strategic fiscal management in difficult times. There is limited academic literature addressing law enforcement cutback management. By gathering existing sources, this document represents a first step in moving the field along from anecdote toward more rigorous cutback management theory.

About the Author

Jane Wiseman is a management consultant specializing in public administration. She served as Assistant Secretary for Public Safety in Massachusetts and was previously Assistant to the Director for Strategic Planning at the National Institute of Justice.

Challenges for law enforcement during times of economic decline

For police managers, several factors make tight economic situations more challenging:

- **Public safety is an essential function of government.** Some government functions can be cut or temporarily suspended to save money. For example, to save money, some government agencies shorten their operating hours. The police, however, cannot simply close one day a week to save money.

- **The success of community policing has elevated public expectations.** Many departments have achieved success in forging bonds with communities through years of proactive policing. That success brings with it the expectation from the community that service levels will remain constant, even in times of fiscal distress.

HELPFUL SOURCES

Excellent examples of police departments using a crisis as a springboard for change and process improvement are found on pages 44-50 in *Good to Great Policing: Application of Business Management Principles in the Public Sector* (http://www.cops.usdoj.gov/RIC/ResourceDetail. aspx?RID=427). This document also provides a quick summary of the business improvement classic *Good to Great* by Jim Collins (New York: HarperBusiness, 2001).

An excellent source for innovative ideas in all areas of state and local government is the Ash Center for Democratic Governance and Innovation at the Harvard Kennedy School. This group gives out annual Innovations in Government awards. Information on its work can be found at http://www.innovations.harvard.edu.

The President has launched a website to share government innovations. Although this is primarily aimed at federal government agencies, some of the innovations leverage technologies (Web conferencing, networked communities) discussed may be useful to police departments. This source of innovative government ideas can be found at http://www.whitehouse.gov/open/innovations.

■ **Collective bargaining reduces discretionary spending.** Personnel is the largest budget item in police departments.[1] When collective bargaining agreements set salary and benefit levels, there is very little discretionary spending that can be cut by an executive. This makes it difficult for a police leader to balance a budget quickly.

■ **Police are not the sole determiners of their budgets, and in a fiscal crisis, top-down decisionmaking may further reduce discretion.** Even without a fiscal crisis, half of police departments report that budget limits are set by the mayor, city manager or finance director.[2] In a crisis, chief executives often want to seize control of the situation. In some cases, governors and mayors make decisions about agency budgets without first soliciting input.

■ **Change is always hard, and it is even harder in difficult fiscal times.** It is human nature to resist change. When change is achieved, it is often because those affected believe the benefits are greater than the costs. In a tight budget, it is hard to make any benefits available, so it can be harder to get buy-in for change. The rewards necessary to inspire cooperation may simply be unavailable.[3]

■ **Morale can suffer.** No one is happy to see their overtime income decrease. Employee spirits are dampened when travel or training budgets are cut. Layoffs, furlough days and loss of staff through attrition can erode institutional experience. Both managers and those in collective bargaining units may experience decreased morale. The result can be decreased commitment to problem solving and creativity. The long-term cost of these intangible losses is hard to quantify but significant nonetheless.

Ways to manage during times of economic decline

The most common approach is to spread budget cuts evenly across an agency or across all agencies in a government. Across-the-board cuts may seem to be fair because they spread the pain. The problem with such cuts is that they do not alter the fundamentals and can often degrade the effectiveness of the agency over time. Across-the-board cuts disproportionately hurt small agencies and efficient operations. Such short-term solutions can result in low morale, reduced creativity and innovation, and stagnation of skills.

The good news and the bad news is that the current fiscal crisis will last a while. This means public agencies will have time to implement lasting organizational improvements. Fiscal stress lasting three or more years has been shown to allow departments time to create new ways of doing business in accounting, budgeting, priority setting for service calls and better resource targeting.[4] These new ways of doing business embody a strategic management approach to budget cutting. Strategic cutback management sets priorities rather than allowing the organization to drift.

Experts on public administration estimate that a budget cut of 7 percent in any one year, or 15 percent over 3 years is about the maximum an organization can sustain and continue to "muddle along" in achieving its mission. If a budget cut of greater magnitude than that is required, strategic management will be needed. When the state of Washington faced a 15-percent budget gap in 2002, the governor decided to try a drastic and different approach to budgeting. An editorial in *The Seattle Times* described the new approach this way:

> The usual, political way to handle a projected deficit is to take last year's budget and cut. It is like taking last year's family car and reducing its weight with a blowtorch and shears. But

Across-the-board cuts may seem to be fair because they spread the pain. The problem with such cuts is that they do not alter the fundamentals and can often degrade the effectiveness of the agency over time.

Strategic cutback management sets priorities rather than allowing the organization to drift.

cutting $2 billion from this vehicle does not make it a compact; it makes it a wreck. What is wanted is a budget designed from the ground up." [5]

The next sections of this report discuss three effective strategies for managing during times of economic decline: Business process re-engineering, performance measurement and budgeting for outcomes. For suggested questions to ask during the strategic cutback management process, see the Appendix, "Key Questions for Effective Cutback Management."

Business process re-engineering

The strategy called "business process re-engineering" (BPR) has come back into the spotlight as a way to save money in lean times. The concept is known by a variety of names: business process re-engineering, business process improvement, business process optimization, value stream optimization and so on. For simplicity, the original term BPR is used here.

The concept first became popular in business but can also help government

agencies achieve better results. One consulting firm expressed it this way:

> In our work with government and public institutions around the world, we have seen incontrovertible evidence that dramatic improvements in performance and productivity can come about when governments make thoughtful, disciplined operational changes. Simply doing the same tasks in new ways, as it turns out, can be extremely powerful.[6]

Numerous examples of how BPR works in the public sector include the following:

- The city of Grand Rapids, Mich., has achieved customer satisfaction despite workforce cuts through consolidating operations, streamlining processes and reducing or eliminating wasted time and effort. The city set up interdisciplinary teams to develop new ways of achieving their work. Each year, the process reaches new agencies.[7]

- The Boston Police Department re-engineered its payroll processing into a streamlined system that can track regular time, sick time, overtime and detail pay. The BPR effort was inspired by a newspaper article that revealed officers were simultaneously collecting sick, regular or vacation pay while working paid detail shifts.

- Montgomery County, Md., cut its accounts payable staff by more than half by giving departments the authority to pay invoices up to $5,000 rather than going through the central accounts payable office.[8]

BPR is defined by Michael Hammer and James Champy, authors of *Reengineering the Corporation*,[9] as "the fundamental rethinking and radical redesign of business processes to achieve dramatic improvements in critical, contemporary measures of performance, such as cost, quality, service and speed." During the 1990s, BPR generated great success in back-office processing, manufacturing and warehouse operations. Today it is coming back to address the economic challenges of the customer-facing side of business. For businesses, this will include product development, sales and marketing.

Helpful Sources

Executives who face the challenge of declining resources can draw on research and experiences others have faced in the past. Effective cutback management starts by asking questions and developing a detailed budget analysis. The Appendix is a guide for starting the process. It outlines the beginning steps and critical questions to ask.

Asking critical questions in the right context with the right focus will result in categories of cutback. The questions provided in the Appendix were used by multidisciplinary teams from across the criminal justice system who discussed how their interrelated missions and functions would be affected by any changes in budget or process. The questions can also be a helpful guide for agencies or for divisions or departments within an agency.

In government, adoption of BPR has been uneven across states, regions and types of agencies. Many opportunities still exist to improve business processes for the better. Sometimes the result will be money savings, other times it will be time savings, and in other cases it will simply mean greater customer satisfaction. The potential for time and money savings are the key reasons that BPR is of interest during the current fiscal crisis as a way to reduce costs or become more efficient.

In the years since the initial publication of their book, Hammer and Champy have come to realize the most important concept of their definition is "process" and that making process the heart of the organization is the key to success. They note that governments often fail at re-engineering efforts primarily because those in leadership positions are not process-oriented but are instead policy leaders.[10] This bodes well for process re-engineering in law enforcement agencies whose leaders often come from the field and understand the basic business processes of the agency.

BPR is best undertaken by a team diverse enough to generate a variety of ideas. This may mean including different levels, different agencies or even complete outsiders who have a stake in the quality of the process. The important questions to ask in a BPR project are:

- What are we doing?

- How do we do it?

- Why are we doing it that way?

- How could we do it differently if we were building the process from scratch today?

Performance measurement

Performance measurement is a management tool used to help get better results by measuring activity and setting targets for desired results. Performance measurement is a way to draw management attention to priority activities of an organization.

Performance measurement is relevant to cutback management as a way to get more value or productivity out of existing resources, and as a way to identify activities that are not meeting performance standards and can be candidates for elimination.

Performance measurement in law enforcement and public safety agencies

Thinking about how to measure performance in policing, in 1992 George Kelling wrote a paper called "Measuring What Matters."[11] In it, he challenged the existing measures of law enforcement (arrests, crime rates) as appropriate ways of measuring the success of community policing efforts. In the years that followed publication of that paper, the National Institute of Justice and the Office of Community

Oriented Policing Services jointly hosted a series of meetings for academics and practitioners concerned with understanding how best to measure success in policing. A research report was published in July 1999 with summaries of the papers presented at the three sessions held to explore this topic.[12]

Various perspectives for measuring what matters include:

- **CompStat at the NYPD.** One of the most well-known examples of performance measurement in public safety is the implementation of CompStat at the New York City Police Department. According to William Bratton, who served as police commissioner in New York City, measuring police efforts is a key to motivation and success. In his words, "Goals become a means not only of measuring success but of replacing unproductive or counterproductive behaviors with effective, goal-oriented activity."

- **Maryland StateStat.** Maryland Governor Martin O'Malley manages state government with numeric data and a policy of accountability for managers to meet performance

HELPFUL SOURCES

In *The Reinventor's Fieldbook: Tools for Transforming Your Government* (San Francisco: Jossey-Bass, 2000), David Osborne and Peter Plastrik provide an extremely practical set of tools for carrying out the work described in *Reinventing Government*, by Osborne and Ted Gaebler. This is a very useful and accessible handbook.

In *Creating Public Value: Strategic Management in Government* (Bridgewater, N.J.: Replica Books, 1997), Mark H. Moore has a chapter on "Reengineering Public Sector Production" in which he compares two case studies, one from the Boston Housing Authority and the other from the Houston Police Department. Using the cases, Moore describes how to define the organizational mission and the product. He then provides advice on how to redesign the production processes, reflecting the fact that police departments are like service enterprises in the private sector in that their greatest cost element is personnel and that the "product" is actually the interaction of those personnel with outside customers. Moore ably addresses police culture, the importance of aligning systems with mission, and the tradeoffs between centralized control and connection to community.

A useful source for information on process improvement is http://www.lean.org. This website is run by a nonprofit organization that provides free Web-based training services and also has a wealth of articles for free and other materials for purchase.

targets. One of the benefits of looking at the numbers is being able to make decisions based on total costs and benefits. For example, a state juvenile detention facility was closed because it was operating at far less than capacity. The total savings was $1.5 million. Of that amount, $600,000 was used to fund less expensive community-based programs that use evidence-based family therapy and education programs proven to be more effective than incarceration.[13]

■ **Massachusetts Sex Offender Registry Board.** The Massachusetts Sex Offender Registry Board is responsible for registering and classifying sex offenders. When then-Massachusetts Governor Mitt Romney's performance measurement initiative was launched in 2004, the agency did not know how many individuals required to register as sex offenders had failed to do so. Simply asking for the basic statistics from the agency was a helpful exercise. But even more helpful was the ability to focus efforts on the most serious cases. When the agency identified those in violation of their registration requirements who were at the highest risk to reoffend, they were then able to engage state and local law enforcement in sweeps to locate and register these offenders.

■ **Sunnyvale, Calif.** When Sunnyvale, Calif., pioneered performance-based budgeting in the 1980s, it established outcome goals for every agency of government. It set nine outcome goals for the police department and each goal was given a weight of one to five depending on how important it was to public safety. "When the police began measuring these outcomes and adding the weights, they realized that domestic violence accounted for 50 percent of the weighted crime. The Public Safety Department then reorganized internally to attack domestic violence more effectively, and it convinced the City Council to spend more on combating domestic violence."[14]

The mechanics of performance measurement

Many law enforcement agencies have already implemented performance measurement for crime statistics, following in the CompStat model. That is well documented in other sources.

When developing new performance measures, one of the key recommendations is to make sure they are "S-M-A-R-T" measures. That means that the measures should be:

- **Specific** — Performance measures need to be precise and clear, otherwise it is hard to understand exactly what they are. For example, "decrease crime" is unspecific. A more specific performance goal is "decrease violent crime by 3 percent."

- **Measurable** — Performance measures and targets need to be things that can be measured. Employee sick days can be measured, overtime expenditures can be measured and number of burglaries can be measured. Vague or general terms like "morale" and "crime" are harder to measure. For any area in which performance measurement is desired, law enforcement leadership should try to find something that can be measured. For example, morale can be measured through employee satisfaction surveys. A proxy measure for morale is often the use of sick time.

- **Attainable** — Setting performance targets that are unrealistic will only deflate morale when they are missed. Attainable goals are inspiring.

HELPFUL SOURCES

There are a number of performance measurement reports that are public and may provide helpful inspiration. Some examples include:

New York City Mayor's Management Report (available online at http://www.nyc.gov/html/ops/html/mmr/mmr. shtml).

City of Portland [Oregon] Service Efforts and Accomplishments: 2008-09 (available online at http://www. portlandonline.com/auditor/index.cfm?c=49566&a=274496).

Prince William County, Virginia, 2006 Service Efforts and Accomplishments Report (available online at http:// www.pwcgov.org/accountability).

An excellent source for examining the philosophical debate on how performance measurement can be used in a law enforcement agency is found in the NIJ publication, *Measuring What Matters: Proceedings From the Policing Research Institute Meetings,* Research Report, Washington, D.C.: U.S. Department of Justice, National Institute of Justice, July 1999, NCJ 170610.

The National Performance Management Advisory Commission published a public review draft in July 2009 of a helpful tool for implementing performance measurement and performance management efforts. *A Performance Management Framework for State and Local Government: From Measurement and Reporting to Management and Improving* (http://pmcommission.org/APerformance ManagementFramework.pdf) provides step-by-step instructions for beginning a performance measurement effort and provides helpful advice and suggestions for the implementing process.

For information on federal performance measurement efforts and for sample performance measurement questions, visit http://www.expectmore.gov. This Office of Management and Budget website provides information to the public on federal programs that have been evaluated using performance measures.

- **Relevant** — Performance measures must connect to core elements of the agency's mission or they are not useful.

- **Time-based** — Performance measures and performance targets need deadlines. For example, "decrease violent crime by 3 percent within one year" is time based. Without a deadline, it will be impossible to determine if the goal is on target or not.

Performance measurement trends

Increasingly in the private sector, organizations are moving from performance measurement to performance management. The difference is in adopting a philosophy throughout the organization that the results — either achieving performance goals or not — have consequences. Management then motivates staff to achieve goals and creates both incentives to achieve and penalties for not achieving metrics. In settings with collective bargaining units, management and unions collaborate to establish the incentives and penalties.

Organizations that use performance measures effectively use them both internally and externally. The look at the external environment is called benchmarking. In "benchmarking," an organization looks at similar agencies and at best-in-class agencies to compare performance. This is a way to ensure that performance targets are aggressive and meaningful.

Budgeting for outcomes

In their book *The Price of Government* (see note 8), David Osborne and Peter Hutchinson argue that the problem with traditional budget cutting is the focus on what is cut and not on what is kept. They argue entities should stop focusing on the 10-15 percent of the budget that gets cut and instead devote themselves to improving the effectiveness of the 85-90 percent of the budget that is kept. They ask, "What value are we getting for our money?"

Their idea brings back memories of "zero-based budgeting" but with a twist. In zero-based budgeting, each program is reviewed with the assumption that it must prove itself in order not to be zeroed out. "Budgeting for Outcomes" looks at the desired end result across all agencies of government, rather than looking at each spending line item in each individual organization. An excerpt from the book summarizes their approach:

> The first step is to turn the budget process on its head, so that it starts with the results we demand and the price we are willing to pay rather than the programs we have and the costs they incur. The second is to build the budget by deciding to buy only those programs that deliver the results we want and leave the rest behind. Then we must cut government down to its most effective size and shape, through strategic reviews, consolidation, and rightsizing; use competition to squeeze more value out of every tax dollar; make every program, organization and employee accountable for results; use technology to empower customers and save money; and reform how government works on the inside (its management systems and bureaucratic rules) to improve its performance on the outside.[15]

One key element of Budgeting for Outcomes is that it is done across an entire government enterprise — a state, county or city. The outcomes desired by citizens often cut across departments, and the budget then is driven by outcome instead of by department. As Budgeting for Outcomes practitioner Roger Neumaier, the Snohomish County, Wash., finance director said, "We do not fund processes: we fund outcomes."[16]

Although the approach is meant for an entire unit of government, the key themes are relevant to a police department — getting more value out of the budget by focusing on what is most important and ignoring organizational silos in pursuit of valued outcomes.

Traditionally, law enforcement agencies have used a line-item budget format. This is the least flexible format for police executives, as the authorizing agency (mayor or city council) determines the budget on a line-by-line basis. More and more agencies are using performance budgeting or mission-driven budget processes.[17]

Although there are challenges to adopting Budgeting for

Outcomes in a law enforcement agency, there are some
elements of the process that
can prove useful. A quick
summary follows.

■ **Set goals.** Budgeting for
Outcomes starts with
defining the goals that are
most important to the community. Specific recom-
mendations in the book
regarding goals include:

– *Adopt a narrow focus.*
The book recommends
keeping a clear focus
and not having too
many goals — 15 is too
many, 10 is good, five
is even better. When
Mesa County, Colo.,
implemented Budgeting
for Outcomes, it identi-
fied 10 priority areas for
government. Multnomah
County, Ore., established
six priorities of govern-
ment for its 2007 budget.

– *Focus on outcomes, not
outputs or activities.* For
example, if the goal is to
reduce gang violence,
police executives should
focus on that, not on
activities such as arrests,
home visits or call out
meetings.

– *Be realistic.* Achiev-
able goals are inspiring;
impossible goals are not.

Police executives should
choose bold but achiev-
able goals.

– *Reach out.* Management
should not set the goals
in a vacuum but should
involve collective bargaining units and other key
stakeholders such as
clergy, community lead-
ers, academics, business
leaders and other justice
system players.[18]

■ **Rank the goals.** All possible budget items are
ranked from highest to
lowest priority based on
the input of the stakeholders. Some cities are using
citizen surveys, town hall
meetings and focus groups
to gather input on what
their community most
values.

■ **Do the homework.** Budgeting for Outcomes teams
search for evidence-based
practices in each goal area.
They look at other government agencies and also
at the private sector for
strategies and approaches
that are effective in getting
results.

■ **Allocate budget dollars
to the top goals.** When
priorities are set, budgeting
can be done by "buying"
the top-priority items and

moving down the priority list until all available funding is spent. In some cases, Budgeting for Outcomes teams "buy" services from other governments or from private contractors if the value is greater than that already provided. In law enforcement, only ancillary services (cleaning, vehicle repair, etc.) are appropriate for this type of outsourcing.

With this structure in place, only the highest priority items are purchased. Any new budget proposals, or proposals to fund something that is below the priority cutoff, must simultaneously propose knocking a higher priority item off the funding list.

An example of Budgeting for Outcomes may help illustrate this process. In Washington state during the 2002-03 budget cycle, then-Gov. Gary Locke needed to trim the budget by $2 billion, which would have required 15-percent across-the-board cuts. Rather than do an across-the-board cut, he chose to focus on the "keeps" rather than the "cuts." He said, "Closing the $2 billion gap we face in the next biennium would require an across-the-board cut of 15 percent — if that's all we did. And that is not what we

are going to do. I don't want to thin the soup. I want state government to do a great job in fulfilling its highest priorities." [19]

The results were impressive. Not only did the governor succeed in cutting the budget and keeping his top priorities protected, but he also achieved recognition from a variety of sources. One newspaper (*The Seattle Times*) called it a "big step forward," and another had this to say:

> Few Washingtonians will find much to like about the brutal state spending plan Governor Gary Locke recommended Tuesday. But as ugly as the result was, there's a lot to like about the way Locke and his staff arrived at it, using a new process that forced hard choices about the core priorities of state government. [20]

Perhaps most important is that the public approved. In a survey, 64 percent concurred with the statement, "Whether or not I agree with all of the governor's budget recommendations, I respect his leadership and vision to solve the current problem and get the state's economy back on track." [21]

Helpful Sources

The most comprehensive source for learning about Budgeting for Outcomes is the book *The Price of Government,* by David Osborne and Peter Hutchinson (see note 5). Other helpful references include:

Government Finance Officers Association, at http://www.gfoa.org, includes helpful information for smaller municipalities to implement the Budgeting for Outcomes approach. An icon on the lower left of their home page links to the sources there, such as a Web-based set of resources and coaching package, including a step-by-step guide to implementation and more than 125 documents that can be used as templates or examples. Information is also available via e-mail at bfo@gfoa.org.

Public Strategies Group, at http://www.psg.us, provides up-to-date information on states, cities and counties that have adopted the Budgeting for Outcomes approach.

One interesting component of Budgeting for Outcomes is "gainsharing." Gainsharing provides a financial incentive for employees to identify savings opportunities. Employees keep a portion of savings they identify or help achieve, either as an individual payment or as an agency allowance.

When Seattle instituted gainsharing for its wastewater treatment operation, over the course of four years, the employees got to keep $2.5 million in savings generated by their ideas. There was no reduction in quality of service.[22]

Gainsharing may be challenging in a law enforcement agency, as the greatest component of cost is personnel. However, there may be opportunities in support services, procurement, information technology or other areas where innovative employee suggestions can create financial savings that can be shared among employees. In implementing a gainsharing program, *The Price of Government* recommends that the amount employees keep be enough to inspire their participation, and suggests 50 percent of the savings may work. They also recommend that the savings be protected from being raided to balance the budget, as this type of "bait and switch" could undermine confidence in the system.[23]

Examples of agencies that have implemented Budgeting for Outcomes do not yet include any (known) police departments. Most of those that have taken it on have done so across all agencies of government. Some examples include Washington state; Iowa; Spokane, Wash.; Denver, Colo.; Dallas, Texas; Fort Collins, Colo.; Azusa, Calif.; Mesa County, Colo.; Multnomah County, Wash.; and Snohomish County, Wash.

Budgeting for Outcomes is becoming a more and more valuable tool now that so many governments find themselves with deficits. It provides a method for being strategic; rather than cutting all programs across the board, this method allows for focusing on what is most valued by the community. It forces agency leaders to make tough choices that are aligned with the strategic plan.

The Government Finance Officers Association (GFOA) launched a program to help smaller communities implement Budgeting for Outcomes with a set of Web-based tools and training, along with some technical assistance for implementation. GFOA hopes to build capacity for the long term, beginning now with the budget crisis as the incentive to change. As the GFOA website says, "In eras of budget constraint or surplus, this new strategy is revolutionizing public sector financial management all across the country."

Selected current approaches

This section of the document describes common cutback management strategies typically used in law enforcement agencies. Approaches for personnel are presented first, as personnel costs are the largest component of a law enforcement budget. Vehicle and technology operations cutback management approaches are also addressed. For each topic, strategic approaches are described, followed by a discussion of short-term approaches that are best used with caution.

Personnel cutback management strategies

As the largest component of any law enforcement budget, personnel costs are a key area to look for savings. Strategic approaches to personnel management with long-term benefit include the following:

- **Proactively managing overtime.** In many departments, overtime can become a huge expense. Research about overtime shows that it can best be controlled by recording, analyzing and managing. Although overtime is an unavoidable cost of policing, it can often be managed better than it currently is. Many police departments do not have systems to record the number of overtime hours used and the circumstances of that overtime. Most departments can produce records for their overtime use, but many cannot document the number of overtime hours used in the last five years. Recommendations for better managing overtime include such techniques as scheduling court appearances during regular work hours instead of using overtime and holding shift supervisors accountable for shift extension overtime decisions.[24] The following two examples demonstrate success and the third presents a cautionary note on proactively working to ensure overtime cuts do not decrease morale:

– The Milwaukee Police Department (MPD) has taken an aggressive approach to overtime management. Through active monitoring, the MPD was able to come in on budget last year for overtime for the first time in 10 years. According to Chief Edward Flynn, before the overtime management initiative, overtime was "spent like water," going over budget each year. By providing an overtime budget to each manager and then holding that manager accountable for managing to the budget, significant reductions were achieved. Prior to the initiative, the City of Milwaukee Office of the Comptroller conducted a study and found that MPD spent more on police overtime than did its peer cities.[25] The largest reductions were in areas where there had been habitual overuse, such as in investigations. Many patrol officers saw no change in their overtime pay and, as a result, morale problems were averted.[26]

– The Massachusetts State Police reduced overtime by 53,000 hours in 2009 and saved $3.3 million. Colonel Mark Delaney attributed this to more careful management by supervisors. A separate initiative has reduced sick time use.[27]

– In Portland, Ore., when a large decrease in overtime was implemented it undercut morale significantly. In fact, "some undercover officers showed their displeasure by dropping whatever they were doing at the moment their shift ended — even while tailing suspects or executing warrants."[28]

Working collaboratively with collective bargaining units will be important to the success of any overtime-reduction effort.

■ **Review employee health care costs.** Employee health care costs can be significant. Increasing the employee contribution to health care premiums is one strategy to consider. This approach may be difficult in a collective bargaining situation, but if successful can achieve savings. Encouraging or requiring eligible retirees to enroll in Medicare for their health coverage can produce large savings. A midsized New England city saved $5 million in 2007 and "at least that much" for fiscal years 2008 and 2009 by enrolling municipal retirees in Medicare.[29] Another strategy is to institute wellness programs that can reduce overall health care costs related to sick time and insurance premiums. Motorola implemented an employee wellness program that saved $3.93 in health care costs for every $1 invested in the program, and when

Johnson & Johnson instituted a wellness program they saved $224.66 per employee per year in health costs.[30]

■ **Supplementing staff with volunteers if possible.** Whether called reserves, auxiliaries, deputies or specials, volunteer citizens are helping as a modern-day "posse" in some law enforcement agencies. In some cases, college interns are providing no-cost or low-cost services that were previously done by civilians. In many municipalities, collective bargaining agreements will make it difficult to replace officer effort with that of volunteers. But if it is possible to do, significant savings can occur. Volunteers save on payroll costs, but do require monitoring and supervision. There are also costs associated with recruiting, training and equipping volunteers. Some examples of the use of volunteers include the following:

– At the New York City Police Department, Auxiliary Police perform uniformed foot, vehicle and bicycle patrols. They are trained to observe and report conditions requiring the services of the regular police. Whenever possible, they assist in nonenforcement and nonhazardous duties. Auxiliary Police assist with community festivals, parades, concerts, street fairs, park patrols, subway entrances and token booth areas, and crime prevention activities.[31]

– In St. Joseph, Minn., 12 people volunteer their time to the Dakota County Sheriff's Mounted Patrol. These volunteers not only donate their time, they also provide their own horses and trailers. They help with crowd control and with searches. Dakota County also has part-time licensed officers who receive the same training as full-time deputies. They make up a special unit, can carry weapons and can make arrests with a full-time officer present. They contribute 2,000 hours of service each year.[32]

– In Green Valley, Ariz., 90 men and women volunteer their time to back up local deputies. They control traffic at accident sites, aid in search and rescue missions, and check houses left empty for extended periods of time such as for summer vacations. The commander of their unit estimates their service saves $1 million a year.[33]

– Jackson County, Ky., saves $250,000 to $500,000 per year with their reserve deputy force. Reserve deputies help with drug busts, security for celebrities, patrol functions at major events, fundraising for a children's charity and speaking engagements at schools.[34]

■ **Disbanding costly specialized units.** In Boston and San Diego, mounted patrol divisions have been disbanded due to budget shortfalls. In San Diego, the horses were sold. In Boston, the department was optimistic and signed contracts to sell the horses with a contingency that the horses be returned if the funding becomes available to support the unit again.[35]

■ **Rethinking staffing and supervision ratios.** In Massachusetts, the state police troopers union is seeking an outside audit of the supervision structure. The group claims that it would be possible to reduce the number of management positions and save $1 to $7 million a year in staffing costs by reducing the number of management positions.[36]

- **Rethinking staffing for public building security details.** In some cities and states, police officers providing building security are being reassigned to patrol duties. In one case, several entrances to a public building have been closed to the public to save on the cost of paying an officer to man the station.

Short-term or one-time cost cutting measures are being used in many law enforcement agencies to close budget gaps. While these measures are common and do solve short-term budget challenges, they are not structural changes and will not have enduring impact. The following measures are not strategic changes and provide only temporary relief from budget problems.

- **Delaying hiring.** Deferring the start of a new recruit class and keeping vacant positions open will produce short-term budget savings. However, when a class of recruits is ready for training but put on hold, some may take other jobs before the class is started. Then when the class does start, it may cost more time and effort to recruit to replace those who have been lost. Delaying hiring is not a long-term fix and should not be the sole method used to close a budget gap. As with other short-term fixes, it may be appropriate to use this in concert with long-term strategic changes.

- **Cutting back on training.** Training is typically among the first budget line items to be cut. This is a short-term fix that can have negative effects in the long run as skills stagnate and morale

HELPFUL SOURCES

For a classic explanation of how to manage overtime, see Bayley, D., and R. Klorden, "Police Overtime: An Examination of Key Issues," Research in Brief, Washington, D.C.: U.S. Department of Justice, National Institute of Justice, May 1998, NCJ 167572. Although this report is more than 10 years old, the principles remain solid.

For an excellent "Fiscal First Aid Kit" with detailed questions to ask for each area of budget cutting addressed in this section, see the Government Finance Officers Association website, at http://www.gfoa.org/index.php?option=com_content&task=view&id=938#goto7.

Free online law enforcement training related to DNA forensic evidence is available at http://www.dna.gov/training.

suffers. Drastic reductions in training levels may hurt certification. Further, to become a more efficient organization, often training is necessary for improved performance. Rather than cut back on the amount of training that is offered, an alternative is to reduce the cost of training. One method is to switch from training that requires travel to training that can be conducted nearby or online. (In addition to online trainings, many organizations are using webinars or webcasts rather than in-person meetings and conferences.) For additional offerings on general management topics, the federal government provides a portal at http://www.golearn.gov with free training courses. Completing training online saves travel funds if not training time costs. Further, if some training time can be shifted from overtime to regular time, that also saves on the training cost.

■ **Encouraging early retirement.** New employees are typically paid less than senior employees. Many states and cities offer early retirement incentives to reduce labor costs. The downside of early retirement is the loss of experience that goes out the door with the retirees. A partial solution to this challenge is to invite retirees to come back part time. Not only is there a savings by having them work part time, there is also an advantage that retirees already have their health insurance paid for so they do not incur that new cost to the agency.

■ **Furloughing days and allowing fewer paid days off.** Whether it is reducing the number of paid holidays or paid personal days off, the idea of getting workers to work more for the same pay is a challenging one. This is a strategy likely to save only a small amount compared to systemic change. Further, it can significantly lower morale. In addition, it may be impossible to execute this strategy in a collective bargaining situation. Employee furlough days present the same challenge. For public safety agencies, furlough days are more common for civilian staff than for sworn staff. Morale can suffer when furlough days are implemented, so this strategy is not recommended.

Force multipliers: Partnerships and technology

Organizational improvements can achieve significant savings through use of partnerships or adoption of new technologies. Some strategies already being used or worth considering in law enforcement include the following:

Partnerships

- **Consider outsourcing for nonessential services where appropriate.** Many police departments have saved money by outsourcing services that can be provided at lower cost by outside vendors. Security concerns will be among the top issues to be considered in any possible outsourcing. However, with appropriate safeguards, outsourcing can be cost-effective for IT services as well as other administrative, facility and equipment-support services.

- **Joint purchasing with another agency.** A fundamental rule of procurement is that larger volume purchases achieve lower unit costs. A joint purchase of technology or equipment with other agencies in the same jurisdiction, or other departments in the region, could achieve economies of scale for the purchase. Compare notes with peer agency leaders to determine if there are appropriate choices that can be made as a group more cost-effectively than as individual agencies.

- **Co-location with another agency.** Coconino County, Ariz., Sheriff's Office and Flagstaff, Ariz., Police Department each needed a new building. They built one together and saved considerable cost by building one facility instead of two separate ones. In addition to the building cost savings, there were also some efficiencies for equipment and personnel. They implemented shared services for communications, records and warrants. Instead of each having a separate graveyard shift dispatcher, they now share one. Joint acquisitions of radios and other equipment saved money and allowed for purchasing higher quality equipment.[37]

- **Increased collaboration with private security.** For communities with a strong existing presence of private security, it may be helpful to coordinate budget planning activities. There may be opportunities to reduce redundancies without creating gaps in service. In many cities, private security provides as much as or more law enforcement protection as municipal police services.

Technology

■ **Review new technology options as "force multipliers."** Any technology that can reduce stress on patrol time will be helpful if the cost of the technology pays for itself in reduced staffing costs. Some technologies to consider include red light cameras, surveillance cameras or other manpower-replacing technologies. Further, manpower-intensive tasks that can be done more quickly with technology should be considered. For example, allowing the public to enter incident reports electronically, and either submit to a police department portal or mail in printed documents, will save officer time.

■ **Link existing data in new ways.** The Chicago Police Department created a way to link existing data from within its own systems in new ways. There were tactical, statistical and administrative files in separate places around the department that were disconnected. It created CLEAR (Citizen Law Enforcement Analysis and Reporting) to link the existing data. The results have been impressive — a 22-percent reduction in violent crime and a 27-percent decrease in homicides. Officers are able to solve crimes more quickly, and can solve crimes that were unsolvable before.[38]

■ **Review vendor service agreements for possible economies.** Often, technology vendors charge an annual maintenance fee for their products and services. Depending on the contract terms, there may be an opportunity to find savings. For example, a software service agreement typically has a cost per license. It may be possible to pay for fewer licenses, or to negotiate with the vendor for a reduced rate after a certain number of years. A number of strategies are explored in the technology purchasing strategy documents prepared by SEARCH for the Department of

Justice. Those materials can be found at http://www.search.org.

- **Review outdated technologies and consider retirement.** The New York City Police Department maintains typewriters as a backup for their computers and also for filling out some forms. The cost of the typewriter maintenance contract has been reported as nearly half a million dollars last year. Eugene O'Donnell, a former officer who is currently a lecturer at The City University of New York's John Jay College of Criminal Justice, calls the typewriters an anachronism — and a waste. He says, "The two places you'd find typewriters are the museum and the police department." He believes that the typewriters create significant efficiency and storage problems for the department, causing extra labor and unwieldy paper trails.[39]

Vehicle cost-reduction strategies

A few years ago, when the price of gasoline spiked dramatically, many departments developed innovative ways to reduce their gasoline costs.

Strategies to reduce overall vehicle costs include:

- **Extending vehicle life with proactive maintenance.** One of the most common strategies employed by agencies during the gas price increase of 2008 was to proactively manage preventive maintenance of vehicles. Some examples include:

  – Developing an automatic "tickler" for each vehicle for when it should receive its routine service. This makes sure that no vehicle slips through the cracks and is not actively maintained.

  – Installing hour meters on vehicles so that preventive maintenance can be performed based on the number of hours a vehicle was running. In the case of vehicles that idle for long periods of time, the number of hours running was a more powerful indicator of needed service than the number of miles traveled.

  – The San Diego Police Department runs bi-weekly, monthly and annual cost reports on each vehicle and vehicle type to look for patterns and to manage preventive maintenance. They track mileage for all vehicles and can reassign a high mileage vehicle from one substation to another if needed. Also, doing 95 percent of the maintenance work in-house saves them money on repairs.

■ **Improving service and reducing costs with outsourcing.** For larger departments, outsourcing the maintenance or repair of vehicles can save money and improve outcomes. For example:

- The Chicago Police Department fleet came under the control of a citywide fleet manager. A parts outsourcing contract saved the city $1 million in 2004 for police-related parts. The city of Chicago turned its entire parts inventory over to a private auto parts firm and pays for parts only as needed. In 2004, the city realized about $600,000 in warranty reimbursements for the police fleet. As a result of efficiencies achieved there are now only 150 vehicles per day out of service instead of

the 200-250 prior to program implementation.

- The New York City Police Department uses outsourcing for selective repairs, purchases extended manufacturer warranties on most vehicles, performs warranty repairs in-house and then gets reimbursed by the manufacturer, and does extensive preventive maintenance.

Vehicle costs can also be saved in the choice of vehicle purchases. This has long-term benefit throughout the life of the vehicles. Various approaches include the following:

■ Lower vehicle and fuel costs by switching to smaller or more fuel-efficient vehicles.

■ Negotiate and prioritize to reduce the add-on costs of customizing new vehicles.

Fuel costs are also saved by being more strategic about the use of vehicles, including driving less, idling less and seeking employee reimbursement for their use of the vehicles.

■ **Handling requests for service by phone when possible.** In Raleigh, N.C., some requests for service are now handled over the phone rather than sending an officer to the scene. The Washington County Sheriff in Virginia also has some requests handled via phone if it is agreeable to the caller. This saves fuel. In Milwaukee, a Differentiated Police Response (DPR) Unit allows injured officers to handle a range of calls for service over the phone. Typical calls sent to the DPR are noise complaints and other situations that can be handled with the officer providing the necessary service via phone.

■ **Lowering fuel costs with less idling.** Some agencies are directing their patrol officers to shut off the engine and walk the beat for a period of time (for example, 15 minutes every hour or 2 hours per shift.) In Las Cruces, N.M., officers turn off cars at calls unless emergency equipment is on. For even greater fuel efficiency, Chesterfield County, Va., officers use smart route planning. They are also advised to turn off vehicles when possible.

■ **Driving less and driving more efficiently.** The

Pennsylvania State Police instituted a policy encouraging carpooling to meetings and using videoconferencing instead of driving to meetings when appropriate. It also recommended taking unnecessary items out of the trunk to make the vehicle more fuel efficient and imposed strict enforcement for tire pressure monitoring.

■ **Employee reimbursement for personal use of vehicles.** The West Virginia State Police instituted a rule to require employees to reimburse fuel costs for traveling to and from contract work sites while using their agency vehicles.

■ **Reduce fuel costs by using agency stations.** The Arizona Department of Public Safety Highway Patrol has asked its officers to fill up at state fueling stations. When officers use commercial sites they are encouraged to seek out the least expensive option.[40]

Looking forward

Drastic budget declines are here to stay. The situation is likely to get worse before it gets better. Police executives are left with no choice but to act, and act boldly. Tinkering at the margins simply will no longer do. Big problems such as this call for big solutions. The time is now to find significant cuts that do not erode core services—and that requires rethinking operations to cut *strategically*.

Notes

1. The Police Executive Research Forum (PERF) conducted a survey in 1998 of police departments serving populations of 50,000 or more. The survey yielded 297 responses, for a response rate of 61 percent. Survey findings are presented in the PERF publication, *Police Department Budgeting: A Guide for Law Enforcement Chief Executives,* November 2002.

2. Ibid.

3. Levine, Charles H., "Cutback Management in an Era of Scarcity: Hard Questions for Hard Times" *Public Administration Review* (March/April 1979).

4. Levine, Charles H., "Police Management in the 1980s: From Decrementalism to Strategic Thinking," *Public Administration Review* 45 (November 1985): 691-700.

5. Editorial, "The First Steps Toward Living Within Our Means," *The Seattle Times,* November 17, 2002. Referenced in Osborne, David, and Peter Hutchinson, *The Price of Government,* New York: Basic Books, 2004: 1.

6. Arnum, Hans, Thomas Dohrmann, John Dowdy, and Allison Phillips, "Government's Productivity Imperative," *McKinsey on Government* (Summer 2009): 2.

7. For more information on the Grand Rapids efforts, see their website at: http://www.grand-rapids.mi.us.

8. Osborne, David, and Peter Hutchinson, *The Price of Government,* New York: Basic Books, 2004: 1.

9. Hammer, Michael, and James Champy, *Reengineering the Corporation: A Manifesto for Business Revolution,* New York: Harper Business, 1993.

10. Hammer, Michael, and James Champy, *Reengineering the Corporation: A Manifesto for Business Revolution,* revised and updated, New York: HarperCollins, 2003.

11. Kelling, George, "Measuring What Matters: A New Way of Thinking About Crime and Public Order," *City Journal* 2 (2) (1992): 21-34.

12. Langworthy, Robert H. (ed.), *Measuring What Matters: Proceedings From the Police Research Institute Meetings*, Research Report, Washington, D.C.: U.S. Department of Justice, National Institute of Justice, July 1999, NCJ 170610.

13. Osborne and Hutchinson, *The Price of Government,* 166 (see note 8).

14. Osborne and Hutchinson, *The Price of Government,* 86 (see note 8).

15. Osborne and Hutchinson, *The Price of Government,* xiii (see note 8).

16. Spray Kinney, Anne, and Beverly Stein, "A Solution for Uncertain Times: Budgeting for Outcomes," *California Counties* (May/June 2008): 10-14.

17. PERF (see note 1).

18. Osborne and Hutchinson, *The Price of Government,* 70-71 (see note 8).

19. Ibid., 6.

20. *The News Tribune.* Quoted in Osborne and Hutchinson, *The Price of Government,* 11 (see note 8).

21. Osborne and Hutchinson, *The Price of Government,* 11 (see note 8).

22. Ibid., 15.

23. Ibid., 250.

24. Bayley, D.H., and R.E. Worden, "Police Overtime: An Examination of Key Issues," Research in Brief, Washington, D.C.: U.S. Department of Justice, National Institute of Justice, May 1998, NCJ 167572.

25. Morics, W.M., *Audit of Milwaukee Police Department Overtime,* Milwaukee, Wisc.: Office of the Comptroller, June 2007.

26. Interview with Edward Flynn, August 19, 2009.

27. Murphy, Shelley, "Troopers Ask Patrick for Audit of State Police," *The Boston Globe,* August 9, 2009.

28. Osborne and Hutchinson, *The Price of Government,* 28 (see note 8).

29. Carey, Robert L., "Controlling the Cost of Municipal Health Insurance: Lessons from Springfield," May 2009, available online at http://www.mccormack.umb.edu/centers/cpm/documents/SpringfieldCostStudy_001.pdf. See also, Massachusetts Department of Revenue (Marilyn Montagna, contributor), "Saving Money on Retiree Health Insurance," available online at http://www.mass.gov/Ador/docs/dls/mdmstuf/Technical_Assistance/Best_Practices/savemoneyretirees.pdf.

30. United States Department of Health and Human Services, *Prevention Makes Common "Cents,"* Washington, D.C.: U.S. Department of Health and Human Services, September 2003.

31. See http://www.nyc.gov/html/nypd/html/careers/auxiliary_police.shtml.

32. Hildreth, R., "Modern Posse," *Law and Order* 38 (6) (June 1990): 30-33.

33. Ibid.

34. Ibid.

35. Collette, Matt, "Boston Police Commissioner Defends Dismantling of Mounted Unit," *The Boston Globe* June 23, 2009, Brown, Steve, "The End of an Era for the Boston Police Mounted Unit, "WBUR 90.9FM, June 25, 2009, available online at http://www.wbur.org/2009/06/25/bpd-mounted-unit; "Police Commissioner's Internal Memo to Department Members," posted March 4, 2009 at http://www.bpdnews.com/?s=FY2010+Budget+Cuts;

Martin, Jeff, "Mounted Police Fading in Sunset?" *USA Today,* February 11, 2010; Kahn, Amina, "San Diego Police Department to Fold Mounted Unit, Auction Off Horses to Cut Costs," *Los Angeles Times,* February 5, 2010; Dudley, William, "Balboa Police Horses To Be Sold at Auction," *San Diego Examiner,* January 6, 2010; Cubbison, Gene, "Put Out to Pasture," *NBC San Diego,* January 8, 2010, available online at http://www.nbcsandiego.com/news/local-beat/Put-Out-to-Pasture-80945972.html; San Diego Police Department press release, January 29, 2010, available online at http://www.sandiego.gov/police/about/media/pdf/2010/100129horsetackauction.pdf.

36. Murphy, Shelley, "Troopers Ask Patrick for Audit of State Police," *The Boston Globe,* August 9, 2009.

37. Chrisinger, Jim, "A Law Enforcement Sharing Story," *Public Management* 92 (4) (May 2010).

38. Wexler, Chuck, Mary Ann Wycoff, and Craig Fischer, "'Good to Great' Policing: Application of Business Management Principles in the Public Sector," Washington, D.C.: Police Executive Research Forum, 2007: 41-42.

39. Kessler, Jason, "Typewriters Live on in New York Police Department," CNN.com, July 13, 2009.

40. LeSage, J., "Cutting Car Costs," *Police: The Law Enforcement Magazine* 29 (4) (April 2005): 42-44, 46, and Gavigan, J., "Rising Fuel Prices Affect Agencies Across the Country," *Law and Order: The Magazine for Police Management* 56(8) (August 2008), 74-76, 78-80, 83.

Appendix: Key questions for effective cutback management

Step 1 — Asking the big questions. The following critical overarching questions of cutback management guide the exercise and address the enterprise as a whole. Working through these questions guides the entire process. Looking at each activity across the enterprise, leaders ask:

- What things can we stop doing?

- What things can others do? (e.g., city, state, county, private agency)

- What things can be done more effectively?

- Where can lower cost labor be used?

- Where can capital or technology substitute for labor?

Step 2 — Conducting detailed budget analysis. For each activity that the organization undertakes, ask the following questions to evaluate whether the cost of that activity can be reduced or eliminated.

Examine organizational mission

- What are the organizational musts or mandates, as defined by statute, funding guidelines, executive order, etc.?

- What are nonmandated organizational functions?

- What activities does the organization do very well?

- What activities does the organization do with less effectiveness?

- Which traditional organizational functions have not recently been examined for degree of fit with the mission?

Examine marginal investments

- What programs have the highest unit costs?

- What programs serve a small or isolated clientele?

- What programs provide services available from other public or private organizations?

- What programs have consistently fallen below their goals or expectations?

- What programs, if cut back, would have long-term pressures and greater future costs?

Install rational-choice mechanisms

- What management tools have been developed to assist managers and policymakers in making rational choices among competing demands?

- Are performance measures available to assess effectiveness?

- What program evaluation techniques have been used?

Improve personnel management

- Have employee inputs been solicited for reduction strategies?

- Do incentives exist to encourage employee participation?

- Have managers openly discussed resource constraints with union leadership?

- Have unions indicated willingness to work with managers to achieve economies?

- Have productivity programs with sufficient incentives been tried or explored?

- Have organizational changes such as consolidation, centralization, decentralization, facilities closing and schedule changes been considered or attempted?

- Once made, are personnel decisions quickly carried out?

- Are some personnel over-qualified or underqualified for the tasks they perform?

- Are some tasks overly simple for the personnel to whom they are assigned?

- Can position reclassification reduce the cost of selected tasks?

- What administrative duties can be transferred to junior personnel?

- What administrative duties can be transferred to civilian personnel?

- What services can be provided by part-time or consultant resources?

- What services can be delivered by volunteers?

- What additional workload can be placed on existing slack resources?

Examine equipment and technology

- Can vehicles or other equipment be downsized?

- What processes can be automated?

- How can existing computer systems be used more efficiently?

- What communications technology can be used to streamline processes or save labor hours?

- Are there items that can be leased rather than purchased?

- Can any service agreements for equipment or technology be renegotiated at more favorable rates?

Improve external relationships

- Has the manager communicated problems to key external stakeholders?

- Has the manager solicited assistance from stakeholders?

- Has the manager kept the political body informed?

- Has the manager kept the public informed?

About the National Institute of Justice

The National Institute of Justice — the research, development and evaluation agency of the Department of Justice — is dedicated to improving our knowledge and understanding of crime and justice issues through science. NIJ provides objective and independent knowledge and tools to reduce crime and promote justice, particularly at the state and local levels.

NIJ's pursuit of this mission is guided by the following principles:

- Research can make a difference in individual lives, in the safety of communities and in creating a more effective and fair justice system.

- Government-funded research must adhere to processes of fair and open competition guided by rigorous peer review.

- NIJ's research agenda must respond to the real world needs of victims, communities and criminal justice professionals.

- NIJ must encourage and support innovative and rigorous research methods that can provide answers to basic research questions as well as practical, applied solutions to crime.

- Partnerships with other agencies and organizations, public and private, are essential to NIJ's success.

Our principal authorities are derived from:

- The Omnibus Crime Control and Safe Streets Act of 1968, amended (see 42 USC §§ 3721-3723)

- Title II of the Homeland Security Act of 2002

- Justice For All Act, 2004

To find out more about the National Institute of Justice, please visit:

www.nij.gov

or contact:

National Criminal Justice Reference Service
P.O. Box 6000
Rockville, MD 20849-6000
800-851-3420
www.ncjrs.gov

The National Institute of Justice is a component of the Office of Justice Programs, which also includes the Bureau of Assistance; the Bureau of Justice Statistics; the Community Capacity Development Office; the Office for Victims of Crime; the Office of Juvenile Justice and Delinquency Prevention; and the Office of Sex Offender Sentencing, Monitoring, Apprehending, Registering, and Tracking (SMART).

www.ingramcontent.com/pod-product-compliance
Lightning Source LLC
Chambersburg PA
CBHW070526290526
45790CB00003B/1314